As Our Fathers Told Us

As Our Fathers Told Us

Religious Poetry in a Post-Christian Age

PLACIDUS HENRY

RESOURCE *Publications* · Eugene, Oregon

AS OUR FATHERS TOLD US
Religious Poetry in a Post-Christian Age

Resource Publications
An Imprint of Wipf and Stock Publishers
199 W. 8th Ave., Suite 3
Eugene, OR 97401

www.wipfandstock.com

PAPERBACK ISBN: 978-1-6667-4821-5
HARDCOVER ISBN: 978-1-6667-4822-2
EBOOK ISBN: 978-1-6667-4823-9

03/27/23

In Honor of the Holy Spirit, Treasury of Blessings.

Contents

Acknowledgements

Gratitude to the following journals for giving these poems homes:

Assisi: "Pearness" & "Dark"

Blue Collar Review: "Bus to Work," "Ode to Enough," Small Working Class Rewards," "Mexicanos," "Reporter's Notebook," & "Quadruple Haiku Plus Two"

Cairn 45: "Ascension"

Friends Journal: "Low-Rent Psalm."

Poetica Vita: "Invitation List"

Presence: "Advent Vespers at New Skete"

Issues: "Shabbat"

Silver Wings: "Deliverance"

The American Dissident: "Economics 101"

War, Literature, & the Arts: "Full Bird in Flight"

Thanks to Ruth Ann LeHane for formatting and typing support.

Introduction

My earthly father taught me to tie my shoes while also teaching me the paternoster. It it was a parable addressed to me, a parable in vignette, of what was to be a life-long pilgrimage in the Spirit. You might call it the beginning step of a long winding road. Other such stepping stones were Catholic teaching nuns, a year set aside for prayer at seminary, spiritual reading and retreats. Then there were years as Catholic, Quaker, and as an Antiochian Orthodox Christian.

Should I count my lapse of twenty years, when like the younger son in Luke 15, I ignored invitations by the Spirit so that I could indulge my whims? Absolutely, the emptiness, confusion, and lost time which ensued was invaluable. Eventually, they made me "come to myself." Before the regeneration, however, I looked back with the same sadness as that of a lover feeling, "she's the one who got away."

Statistics tell us, that right now, 15 to 20% of young people are departing from most churches. They may eventually repair the relationship, as Luke's wayward son once did, after opening the gaily wrapped gifts the world offers. Or not. I ran a spiritual awareness group on a hospital's behavioral unit and was shocked by the way modern culture has drowned or distracted the wisdom of the past. One intelligent young man thought that the gods of Greek mythology were part of an active religious system. Others were terminally confused, looking for any path to walk.

Pastors proffer remedies of youth camps, children's liturgies, and Sunday School. Professors suggest contextual theology, a more academic form of "meet them where they are at." These are recycled methods for a complex new reality, the condition of post-Christianity. Pledges to a two thousand year old faith grows fainter in the face of a triumphant secular-technological culture based on the philosophy of "me-firstism."

The hunger for meaning is deep in our youth. Faith leaders often miss the saints in their own pews because they don't act like conventionally proper members. I think of a young woman in the group, roundly dismissed because she heard the Spirit in forest and wished to be married at the ocean. Her moral goodness shone in her face; she was a leader in every corpuscle of her being.

Values of freedom and democracy must be part of an American spirituality, nevertheless, our hyper-individualism and "do your own thing attitude" vies with obedience that leads to the righteousness of Rom 1:16. Led by the Spirit, Christianity has had to acclimatize to every seasonal ethos for two millennia. An ancient Church needs the vibrant hope and vitality of such youth. Young people desire a direction, but not to be talked down to. They seek movement along a path to personal progress, not canned instruction. They deplore hypocrisy of any kind. They often need to find their own way.

The simplest path for humans to reclaim what was lost to us is to reexperience its return. A poem can be a memory device. These poems are organized in five clusters: youthful love; work; service (military); social justice; God business. Think of them as free rides to another plane. May they give you pleasure. May the Holy Spirit meet you on the road.

An Intelligent Christian's Basic Book Shelf

The Holy Bible, New International Version, NIV Life in the Spirit Study Bible. Edited by Donald C. Stamps. Grand Rapids: Zondervan, 2003.

Lossky, Vladimir. *The Mystical Theology of the Eastern Church.* Crestwood, New York: St. Vladimer's Seminary, 1976.

Pseudo Macarius. *The Fifty Spiritual Homilies and The Great Letter.* Translated and edited by George A Maloney. Mahwah: Paulist, 1992.

Moltmann, Jurgen. *The Way of Jesus Christ: christology in messianic dimensions.* New York: HarperCollins,1990.

Nolan, Albert. *Jesus Before Christianity.* New York: Orbis, 1992

Otto, Rudolf. *The Idea of the Holy*, Translated by John W. Harvey. London: Oxford University Press, 1950.

Pannenberg, Wolfhart. *Theology and the Kingdom of God*, edited by Richard John Neuhaus Philadelphia: The Westminster, 1977.

Pinnock, Clark H. *The Flame of Love*, Downers Grove, IL: Inter-Varsity, 1996.

Ascension

Still as monk before choir
a great blue heron stands at dusk,
feathered mass on long straw legs,
planted in mud
awaiting a moment of grace.

Day and fish are gone.
No moon yet,
nor star to guide a cowled-ascent.
Obscure shapes collect
along the bank.

Bending a bit he makes a bow
to shadowy figures near the shore,
then more a dancer about to soar,
begets a leap of faith,
takes flight as simply as one would draw a breath
or hold a hand at night.

Pearhood

She bends over a garden of photos
on the floor, planting a picture of rose
and pear here, smiles to encourage us
to seed our consciousness and grow there,
lengthening the vine of creation.

She thinks about helping her students
to open, to ripen. recalls a line
from Rumi's work that makes her stop and wonder,
that impels our own inner rumination.

There are more pears to pick, lemon-tinted,
pale fruit drizzled in early sunlight,
autumnal pulpy sweetness to taste.
She, filled with yellow spring knows that
everything about her past is present
in her face, yet unread,—thresholds, doors, roads.

Her smile is solar; such brightness could banish.
The class mills about looking for answers.
I sit with my notebook, verse lost on tongue.
The class is the stanza, she the poem.

City of Churches

We were proud to be "the "bums" back then
when Brooklyn was the city of churches.
Irish-maids built parishes between subway-
stops with change from the bottom of purses.
Pastors "begot" steeples higher than their neighbors.'
Their parishioners won overseas trips,
courtesy of the United States Army,
staying on at *Colleville-sur-Mer, St. Avold,*
or the Luxembourg American Cemetery.

We grew to idolize those tutored
in privilege: Buckley; Sheen; JFK.
Altar server, I traded cruets,
parleyed with priest in Latin,
blessed myself at foul lines.
I fasted on Fridays in Lent, avoiding delis
with their wheels of pecorino Romano
hanging from the ceiling like Judas.
Walked past pot-bellied barrels of olives,
kosher pickles steeped in brine.
I sought success in the larger world,
asked whether there was a spirituality
of worldliness.
Did the ease of going along, somehow
transmute external facts into internal grace?

Or rather in the way of Teresa of Calcutta,
once a private school teacher charmed
by love of a city's poor,
would it take a forfeiture of will,
seasons of prayer marinating in Spirit,
to transform a random Brooklyn gherkin,
as the gospel might say, into tangy kosher pickle,
thereby, shunning the pallid path of the cuke.

Altar

Together, it was a happy day, crisp
Saturday, shopping for a marriage bed.
Deciding on a futon, king-sized,
as their hopes.
They heaved it up three flights of stairs, laughing.

At Easter liturgy, married a year,
the fringe on the altar cloth reminds her
of the set of sheets she got at shower
from her addled grandma, who had loved her
ever since she could remember.

White carnations crowd the sanctuary,
wounds of red roses poke out
from amid them.
Potted lilies seem to bow their heads
to bread and wine offered there.

A Father Meditates on His Child's Baptism

You cry in surprise as he spills cool drops
across your feverish brow, which burns
like wastelands beyond the Jordan,

at His baptism, "to fulfill all righteousness."
We try, my daughter, to screen sand
from eyes and impede the demon's work.

Isaiah promised a desert gushing water,
parched lands that grow the crocus,
blistering ground that blooms and bubbles with joy.

Jesus pledged more than nice behavior,
offered a treasure in a jar of clay,
spoke of streams of living water, springing up in us,
            for which he'd dearly pay.

To me, my daughter, you are ceramic without price,
carrying the Spirit as a precious ark.
Bear this water, my daughter, it will
douse us all with grace.

Inside

An insider knows the password,
a word consisting of numbers:
lowercase digits . . . upper case;
at the least, 8 characters strong.

Encrypted inside her belly,
at a minimum for 9 long months,
a Rip van Winkle somnolence, is undressed.
Voyeurism by sonar.

This new life will soon join the parade.
What ribosomal RNA
will set in motion another
character in search an Author?[1]

---

1. The dramatist, Luigi Pirandello, possibly suggests in *Six Characters in Search of an Author* that characters in the play will remain "unfinished" without its creator.

Communion

Milk and eggs, butter and cream are same
In bread or brioche—no difference, really.
Yet nuptial cake placed in mouth of lover,
or slices stored in bedroom closet for years,
(Anniversaries of devotion) are changed

for all time—transfigured you might say.
That meaning of cake transformed,
on mountain matches marvel of disciples
whose master unexpectedly shone like sun,
then simply returned to normal.

Why is this dimension missed by most,
when mystic-witnessed, just an eyelid's width away?
Where is the Spirit who makes this vision
possible for all of us? She who loves the hungry
and the hunger of the world enough to fill it?

Valentine Ghazal

When I met you, my world was so dry it hissed this thing called love.
My family, friends and buddies all dismissed this thing called love.

Our life is one vast vat of greed—unwise lusting.
We turned a curdled ethic into abyss, this thing called love.

We've lived in a surreal time of sex among the ruins.
Porno stars, adult film vendors diss this thing called love.

Many believe in Supreme Being, that God is love.
Mothers, mystic-poets, out-bliss this thing called love.

Your dark hair and deep eyes framed your smile for me.
I worried that it would go amiss—this thing called love.

Like whirling proto-planet you towed me in your orbit.
Mute, why can't I feel out loud, with heart and lips, this thing called love?

Mouth-to-mouth we cannot speak. Our hearts must do this for us.
Let's unpurse our lips, make a tryst, kiss this thing called love.
With you so close, I go about my life placidly;
Remiss, should I lose you. Liable, I'd miss this thing called love.

Bus to Work

Sharon sits astride boulder-hips,
leans toward gran, fishing for coins.
Cleaning women stand at grab poles,
swerving at curves & seem to "walk
their hands up bat"—a sandlot rite.
Packing plant workers, kid in love
with green-eyed girl, they are the same
work-week folk on nursing home route.
Except guy whose Mercedes is
still at garage.

We all share same smell of hot oil,
over-heated muffler exhaust,
sweaty clothes, and sore feet.
The shifts over, each nurse's aide
that day will bring clinic air, they
share at work to homes,
and everyone, as though using
the same lung, will ride the bus
all the way to the end of the line.

Low-Rent Psalm

Yahweh,
you are my umbrella
in thunderstorm,
fleece-lined boots in the great blizzard.

Was it You Who
did not zip past
as I hitched
on the New Jersey Turnpike,
but picked me up
amid the vehicles whizzing by
in the drizzle.

I feel your presence near
so why my hesitation now?
Why my cold doubt at this most electric moment
when the world is about to give me the once-over,
and sings in my ear
of what a good time we'll have?
Sure, I already knew
your priorities, what loyalty is
and what it is not.
There have been enough wreckages
in my own life for me to sense the next one.
You are always close by, my God,
we just don't know where or when.

Up ahead a rusted '90s pickup
flashes its headlights twice,
as I stand at the side of the road
my thumb raised in the air,
shifting back and forth.

Economics 101

I've got mine—too bad for you.
Tax law loopholes were drilled for me,
so that the Deity assures my revenue.

I hire illegals and why not?
Is your sweat worth a penny a pound
   and nights on a cot?

This oil's been bought with a pigmy's purse
and your patriot-son's extra help;
I'll sell you some to gas his hearse.

You get the picture why go on?
Church, court, cop and rep all
get theirs to maintain the con—
    too bad for you.

Making It

On the way up there's always someone for a drink.
Bank teller's Rapunzel-hair is down for your account.
Have a nice day, they'd say afterward.

Since crash, I rent room in this phantom inn.
Before, my doorman would beam and open door;
now with news I'd moved out, he looks away.

Nowadays the only laugh is the clerk flirting
with boyfriend on phone, voice clinking
like martini glasses or high notes

from a lounge piano. My mind skips back
to high school and a teacher's nasal chant
of *Ozymandias* in English class.

He'd try to instruct us in the difference
between the meanings of connote and denote.
One smartass kid said, "What's the connotation
of the verb to die—what has to include things
you once lived for?"

Execs are soldiers, take land at all costs.
Great mastery can be a dirty business.
Statues to success degrade quickly,
faster than stone in a desert.

Winners, don't forget to wash your hands.

Small Working Class Rewards

Here's to those who work in snow and rain,
to shoulders that bring chairs up stairs
and push couches through the air,
notwithstanding gravity.
Here's to those who face their own stress,
no room to cave; no other place to go.
Just like Greek god Atlas, forced to stand
with vaults of heaven on his neck.
Let's give a standing 'o' for elbows' "yes"
to lug-nut's "no," which by ratchet twist
and short swear, changes tire.
Bless the mail carriers who might guess
our private sins from return address.
Forget free turkeys from the past;
give instead a living wage
so, no kid has to fast.
And let's hear it for the biggest prize of all, no doubt,
the chance to put piston rings on kid's old boat
so that we can chase some fattened trout.

Flora in Conversation

Autumn entered the city covertly that year.
The community of low-end window box florets

always pointed it out to older bloomers on 4th floor
of high-rise and laughed at dull uptown Calla Lilies

for once snubbing them. Marigolds and begonias formed
bonds, even living together despite the gossip.

The owner of the building, a hedge fund manager,
vacationed in the Dominican Republic.

He'd wanted to flip the property for office space.
One renter, a window washer from Kiev,

envisioned a future in Wall Street glass soot,
and dreamt of his daughter as a ballerina.

Her *pointe shoes* punched the wooden floor of practice room
deep into night. A young refugee from Ohio

smitten by her in a major way, saw her trash,
almost as collectables, and hauled it away for them.

Marigolds and begonias caught it all.

They saw him study her twirling in mound of leaves,
arms akimbo, body as curved as a longbow.

When the building owner was discovered on the *Playa Rincon*,
ankle chained to anchor under an overturned skiff,

the kid was hired as janitor, then manager-on-way-up.
It was around time he'd taken exam for post office.

That night he dreamed of orgasmic *pointe shoes.* The dancer
moved to Tulsa to audition for company there.

As new postman, he crashed a party
at Eighth Avenue high-rise & watched streets flooding.

A bartizan-like mailbox loose in water surprised him,
sometimes it looked like turret from the ironclad, *Merrimack.*

In it contracts, lading slips, bills of sale,
all the detritus of a throw-away society.

Ode to Enough

Will we ever have enough again
Of supermarket sales with burdened shelves,
Of truckloads and truckloads of high-end stuff,
Or just remain empty men

Dreaming of yellow Humvees, gas tanks full,
That storm city traffic like militias
To reach snowed-in cabins with brand new gear,
Or drive 10 miles for coverlet of wool?

Will not earth again be at our command
To deepen landfills seen from space,
Seek burial grounds proud to keep our trash,
Uproot forests for suburbs on demand.

Now that our many lakes lay drying
Strong stock positions in water slake thirst;
To thrive, markets trade seashore plots, since less is more,
Even though a thirty-ounce quart is still lying.

The ever-curving wheel gives neither more
Nor less to land or sky, but fairly to each,
A radial symmetry of motion.
Unlike the Roman banquet before,
When wealthy feasters puked on waiter-slaves
To unload their burden of sufficiency,
Enjoying again what they just disgorged.
Big Wheels don't have limits, it isn't their mode,

But Demos must fix flat to eat; they know and share the road.
Chauffeurs pay more taxes than the boss,
Pick up his cleaning, take his kid to school.
Demos fixed those wagon wheels that bore a nation's load.
　　Who starves may query, "Will there be enough?"
　　The rest can surely live without the fluff.

Friday in America

sweet grown grass in a Wyeth work hides
fecal droppings near the barn. the falling apple
can't preserve a sense of nature's order,
with chicken coop on fire or murderer
passing through. urban landscapes grow
clichés of business deals above the heads
and behind the backs of the rest of us.
before quick drink and Friday rush home
civil war goes on from tinted suv windows
a suicide's bullet makes the same point:
something is just not working now.

Thanks for Your Service

Young men go off to war
hoping to be heroes,
forfeited legs the crowd applauds
and honors on the talk shows.

Now at home in his car—
the condo where he dwells,
the blood he pledged for country's cause
is the blood he often sells.

While away, day by day,
the country was subverted,
not by spy or espionage, but by
corporate god converted.

They hide their profits overseas
until tax-free they're deeded,
tell oligarchs: we'll waive all fees;
buzz our troops if needed.

Fallen

The obscure
d
r
o
p
unnoticed amid the myriad:
[1.] droplets of rain light
on grass-tips totter
then slide on sheath
beneath layer of soil;
[2.] minute shards
of raised wineglass-dust
smashed on floor
the night before;
[3.] an orphaned vet
brought in casket
to his ultimate
hiding place.

Tuning into the Apocalypse.

watermelon chunks
bludgeoned to death
a torrent of liquid-pulp
       d
        r
        i
        p
        s
on lips and chin.

     s   c   a
  a   d
c   o   e
    f

Gallagher[2]-gouged
gourd-burst
in well-lighted studio.

unlikely seer.
before TV,
prophets, jesters, clowns, barons,
all watchmen of their nation's wreckage,
regularly bellowed truth to deaf-mute kings.

2. American comedian whose TV show featured smashing watermelons
with sledge hammers.

prophesy again.
prophesy with sledgehammer.
prophesy upon the squashed melon,
once oversized and delicious
with flesh and seed to spare,

now splattered and disorganized on the floor,
a cloven empty chamber
like remnants of hatred from an IED.

duck, unhelmeted,
a convulsion is here.
if imperial power,
or frivolous videotape can't redeem,
that cute plum umbrella won't hide us.

Sun Bonnet Sonnet

What is it about us that Hollywood
makes kilos of cash on happy endings?
Was news of the World Trade Center's collapse
a secret in stars' posh sushi bars,
first responders coughing blood into towels?
The vexed viewer knows no resolution now.
We transport high school grads, air freight only,
and return them to us in body bags. Still,
      miracles happen off-screen when they can,
      and failure is compost heap for later
      tries. Francis of Assisi had an eye
      for St. Clare, a townie, who might have said
      "Frankly, I like your style, but let me go,
      I'm on a different flight path."

Full Bird in Flight[3]

Now as dawn-bird dreams out loud
I am at least half awake.
It knows something, even before light slinks
around the corner and warns of morning.
It is a feathered prophet that cries,
"Arise, it's here. Advance."
Movement is life.

All-night TV airs Ailey Company,
first, as teens breakdancing on a corner.
In theater they are coiled springs loving
the arch of each spine.
Their legs bear a good weight; knees propel.
Umbrellas Up! The Sunday parade,
in live slow mo,' high steppin' with the saints.
The sacred circle moves in place.

Light murmurs its definition of the contour of things:
empty water glass;
sand ridges of rumpled covers on my bed at dawn;
pill dispenser;
In my head there is a noise near Syrian border—
I resist the urge to roll away.

All movement is holy. The child's
carousel ride after school is no less joyful

3. Army slang for full colonel, a commissioned officer just below the rank of
brigadier general. The insignia looks like an enlarged eagle with outspread wings.

than the stallion's race is,
or the sudden pivot of starlings in autumn.
Nor the pummel of early spring rain
upon the earth, drops that open it,
and spread it like liquid fingers,
seeding the grass between nearby saplings.
Nor is the sudden splay of flamenco
finger-fan across a dancer's face vain.
All are holy.

Light drizzles on me between Venetian blinds.
I can almost see that boy who
once jogged Vermont hills behind his home,
and later ran an op from chopper in Mosul.
The explosion under me sounded muffled
like popcorn-burst in microwave.
Everywhere I go now I ride, not walk.

Last week, I dreamed buddies broke some roof tiles
to make an opening and lowered my cot
with two olive tow straps—
easy, as though they could do more damage
to my back. Even this simple
aerial maneuver seemed satisfying,
both parachute jump and burial.

There, Jesus sits teaching a crowd.
"You too, Master, were a casualty
of politics and religious warfare.
Make me walk again," I say, "let me kneel."
"You will walk again with me," he says.
"Hooah!" my buddies shout.
. . . "Walk once more in Paradise."
Oh,
I only
hope.

The Vision Thing

Heat peels from back in barracks like a scab.
Should he defect to Turkey with Mahmud?
Too late—Bashar's police know of sick parents.
So, he is assigned to barrel bomb Aleppo,
mix sarin precursors in Al Gouta.

He prays:
"May my father die asleep in his bed.
My own birthday wish: only to see thirty years.
Also: that Mahmud's wife, Fatima, delivers
a healthy child for them. Inshallah".

Fatima's child hesitates as if in thought,
quietly reserves decision to breathe.
Midwife slaps buttock, signals start of race,
but girl holds out, perhaps for better deal.

In Ghouta death is colorless, odorless—
seeps under transom, makes itself at home,
blind to necessities of war.
It spreads, looting supply of oxygen.
The infant reverses decision to live.
          Curious, that an opthalmologist
          can't see what darkness he's achieved.

Stasis in Places

The earth is scuffed with death camps and mass graves,
with infrastructures of injustice and punishment of innocence.
Dictators and oligarchs reign underground;
over a field of snow, black headstones pop up like burnt toast.

A teacher once preached from mountain side,
"Don't retaliate. Do justice." Just this.
Upon his death, the ground shook.

We have been stuck in the current moral space
a long, long time. We have our leaders to thank.
Buried and unremembered, their charred lives
are archived in our common waiting area.

Mexicanos

Mayan ancestors, to go to paradise
must migrate first from hell, from *Xibalba*,
a dark place where winners of Pok-a-Tok
lose their lives and vernal trees die.

There is a collective muscle memory
of digging dry clay earth under the sun,
driven by whip, stalled by heat.
For centuries—rented brown skin.

That sun does not belong to the viceroy,
nor campesinos to the king.
Brown skin belongs only to its wearer,
as a tongue is to its song.
This too is centuries old.

Hesed for the Timid

Nothing so coldly weighs the life of man
as a headstone of the non-dissenter.
He was here once, but now he's gone—
lived among us, but merely as a renter.

He would often hide his voice in that place
where songs are never sung, poems rarely made,
where courage burrows and fears to leave a trace.
He lived most quietly, in short, he was afraid.

To keep himself warm through winter seasons,
he ordered crematoria coal, a role
assigned to him and for no other reasons.
After, he searched, but never found his soul.

Yet to our nature Yahweh is not blind;
he knows some are strong; some are weak.
God's nature is to be kind.
Us? We play games, of hide go seek.

Girl in Mumbai

In the village the people blamed me
when my husband died
four months after we married.

I was 17, four months pregnant
so took work
as servant to business man.

I'd go into boutiques
to feel bolts of cloth
until shopkeeper told me to leave.

Now I stand outside saree window
allowed to press head on glass
so silkworm afterbirth knows no shame
from my skin.

The Pallor of Whiteness

Even in the sunlight, he is a ghost.
I could hold him there, tie him to a post,
but he would slip away like fog to boast
of all dirty tricks, the one he liked most.

I could hold him there, tie him to a post,
let the witches have their way with him
and all his dirty tricks, one he liked most.
His skin offends, has pallor of lepers.

Let the witches have their way with him.
Nazis would know how to make use of it;
his skin offends, has pallor of lepers.
No African should be so pale—doesn't fit.

Nazis would know how to make use of it.
Witches would use albino skin for potions.
No African should be so pale—doesn't fit.
Use his body parts to lift the curses.

Witches used albino skin for potions.
They are good for cheap amulets, at most.
Use the body parts to lift the curses;
even in the sunlight he is a ghost.

Yayoi's Room

(On viewing museum installation, *Repetitive Vision* by Yayoi
Kusama.)

I enter her parallel cosmos conscious
of exclusion from the sorority
of white manikins with Asian face
who tread a mirrored cave gravity-free.
Cool harem of perfect platonic breasts
with blood-spots dropped from a great height
and bare lithe limbs unable to dance,
spied only under recessed black light.
We saunter through this chamber daily
stride past iconic blood and breast, through door
marked private—though laughing gaily—
where women are part trophy, part decor.
And yet it is her power of assent,
the acceptance these mirrors always yield,
that proves more potent than denial and
more frightening than the knives we wield.

Sampling Neighborliness

5-year-old-platinum blond
Carl from deutchland stared
across demilitarized
zone over our backyard fence
wanting, oh so much,
to make us understand
his solemn preschool wish
to be friends with these
big Irish-American kids,
his forehead scrunched,
tongue locked like Zechariah's.
our Seabee uncle
had run into his exploding house,
Carl in bathtub,
to shut furnace down amid flames,
& after he took his bows
as a member of the greatest
generation, laughed at his cancer & died—
with expression as fateful as faces in *American Gothic*[4]
where a farm couple
imperturbably stares down their fortune,
believing *good fences make good neighbors.*[5]

4. A painting by Grant Wood.
5. This and next quote from Robert Frost's *Mending Wall.*

that November a recent widower
made a Thanksgiving
for 2 kids stuck in apartment
over college break
one pre-med & one a drummer
in a grunge band.
last year's break drummer had gone south
on a Mexican road trip
found a bar over the border
with good music & tamales
though he spoke little Spanish.
didn't talk much at all really,
his bandmate once said, his forearms
did all the talkin' he needed.
in bar he first noticed the short wiry guy
wearing a Soundgarden T-shirt,
"cuchara masculino" this guy says
stabbing his camisa with thumb.
"yes, Spoonman," I say.
watching my Yankee jersey with optimum hope
he started to play shirt-charades,
& mimicked pulling Spoonman shirt off his chest
& handing it to me while pointing to
Mickey Mantle's #7 on my back.
"Something doesn't like a wall," I recall
bare-chested in bar, we traded shirts.
In my head the lyric:
"all my friends are brown and red."

Reporter's Notebook

They spilled from a trail out of mountains.
Got the girl a menstrual pad from backpack;
dropped them near my interview location.

Later picked them up again on road
toward caravan. Her head was shaven.
Hermano showed blister-bubble on foot.

Shy at first they told their halting story.
El jefe prowled around her after *quinceanera,*
when watchdog was killed on their farm.

She had thick hair, black as anthracite
Soft as tassels hung in lover's boudoir.
Of course, such gifts are saved for dudes.

She said *Flor de izote* vines reminded
her of three clusters of white flowers she saw
as paths for her: mother; teacher; singer.

El tipo viewed her back like poppy field,
used her hair once to dry his sweaty arms!!
Dude, how caring!!!

That night *madre* shaved girl's head, packed knapsacks
and called a cousin in Arizona.
They joined the caravan in Pecos,
Hands in prayer said, "No names, please. *"Por favor."*

Ribbon Factory

Once we were pooled in the same bloodline,
twinned in one belly, fed by a single spoon
issuing into, lustrous, silky thread,
plush, velutinous.

But threshed, we were broken apart, severed.
Separated from myself, I cursed fate,
and was picked to be a crushed black,
velvet ribbon.

Separation is an old story,
absent space between paired bond,
sensation of phantom limb.

Yes, we've been divided before.
They sold Daddy once to cut tobacco
instead of gather cotton.

My double, my dyed off-white, brother,
was exported to Krefeld, Germany.
The last night I saw him he was a curled
ball of angel-hair in a tired migrant lap.

Sent by freight ship to the Congo,
I made my home among the Kuba people.
Such is the intersection of history and identity.

Quadruple Haiku Plus Two

Prison cells require renters,
        black/brown skins welcome.
Innocence no obstacle.

KKK tactic: use
        of clean laundry to cover
arson, redline and lynching.

Flint water undrinkable.
        Poor folks told it is
fine for brain damaged kids.

My life an old wheelbarrow
        filled with memories—
election votes uncounted.

Going by limo, not bus,
        relaxed no fuss;
I never have to make room.

We defective pens
        flow over paper jerkily.
At end, whose word scratched?

Deliverance

Ps. 18:16

Watch the undercurrent just below
the surface. Note the swirl, the suck
at your knees. The mighty river
is towing you
out to sea.

The rip current knows you too well.
It is in control. It is a
liquid sickle that will cut and drag
you into the swirl and harvest
you like kelp.

Allow it to take you nearer
shore. Hope for gift of tide's
release. See the open door,
the gate ajar. Then before you're lost,
go for it.
Only churn sounds turn in ear.
Feet are flippers and head is bowed.
The waters are parting before you,
as field would yield before reaper.
Ground!!!

Advent Vespers at New Skete[6]

Earth shifts gears downward like a Buick lurching
along an old logging road.
In Holy Wisdom Temple, above iconostasis,
the Logos waits among cerise seraphim
in a muted golden field
the color of tallow-glow.

Shepherds begin their evening fast,
until three tiers of bells sound,
freeing a lupine gene to croon
the contrapuntal call to prayer,
while dusk thirsts for its last drink of light.

Creation joins the common clangor,
as calendar notes the shortening days.
Nature marks the waiting manger,
while a snarling mastiff brays.

As wind finds a place among the mountain choir,
light withdraws along its given path,
filling valley with viscous hours.
Only evergreen pines stand and bow throughout the night.[7]

6. Monks at New Skete support community by breeding, training and sell-
ing German Shepherd dogs.

7. Throughout Orthodox Christian liturgy there are formal and spontane-
ous signs of cross and bows.

To an Atheist Friend

I cannot convince you, my doubting friend
how I relate to an unknowable Being
who can't be introduced at will.
The Easter bunny effect you say.
But we trust the contents of our lives
to digital ghosts in a cloud, or to tangled
fiber optic cables under sea.
My reference is the gospel which deals
with the reality of ears too dull
to hear, the touching of wounds, the taste of life.

Of course, there are other fine books,
Great Expectations by Dickens, i.e.,
in which a secret offstage sponsor emends the plot
of one's life with simple resolution.
Like a step-dad who is an easy touch,
even though he's doing it for your mom.
Sacrifice today is of course *passe;'*
and gods now are neuronal events, yet
for me, my God's glory is
in His felony conviction.

On Getting Miro's *Red Sun*

On first sight Miro's *Red Sun* burned into my soul,
the way bath soap gets into kids' eyes,
the way a cardinal-red-sun trundles into playroom.

It has been years since I stirred with new eyes.
In gallery I am star-climber & bug catcher again,
gaping at sky through Moorish window.

Muddled shapes now evolve into cat-buddah.
Hound dog is huffing ground in harlequin.
Are cherubs shooting marbles with planets?

Age can exile awe, fade its color like bleach
if you let it.
Yet art is a gift of the Spirit.

To get Miro is to find a child's mind again,
that tiny flashlight beating back the night,
an unswaddled light which grows to be naked
and is as penetrating as the noonday sun.

Monday

The vicar's wife folded duvets
and placed them in the armoire
that she received on her wedding day.
The sun streamed as usual through
organza curtains. Dishes
still had to be rinsed and put away,
phone calls made.
The bookcase should be dusted too
and the cross as well.
She misses the last vicarage they had.

God Fatigue

It is said nowadays
that faith is
as unreliable as a button
worn once too often,
with its tired threads separating
from a beloved tweed jacket,
allowing it to pop with the last pound gained.

In this metaphor button is sect,
thread every living tie that binds,
jacket a second skin
that warms whomever needs
its worsted cover.
Nothing else quite fits as well.

Jackets wear in time,
this one fleeced, pierced,
must be patched,
not thrown away
as though it never served,
or saved.

The collar, recalling submission
of master to Master,
of wool cut from back of sheep
gift of ewe and lamb
holds all together
to canopy the soul's decision,
not to nullify the heart's position.

Near Death

The device nurse pored over her patient—
my pacemaker. Tested galvanic current.
Continued flow showed flicker of life-spark,
in its indefinite procession in time.

I feel the circuit delay in me, laze.
Flow in brain turns turgid, lags. Gasp for breath—
a cephalic apnea. Fear seizes me.
I cross the ghat,[8] then revert. I'm back.

I have approached the eternal quiet,
and stumbled backward into time, another
year to watch sallow skin fog mirror.

8. In India a *ghat* is a series of steps descending into the river. It has various uses in addition to entering the river for ritual cremations, for instance.

Dark

(after Jane Kenyon)

An aging barn stands alone . . .
used to have a cross on roof.
Many families of mice started there
on the sweet-smelling hay at night,
though owners preferred rabbits to rodents.

Now, six inch planks slackened, squeak.
As expected, dark and fog oversee the night.
Yet through prevailing cloud reflected,
a two hundred- thousand-mile trip
ends through ill-fitting cracks
that still play their part,
as loopholes for the light.

Tidal Cycle Song

Inside screened porch of nursing home

moon
                                    keeps me company at
                                                        dusk
while parched marsh is replenished.

The second shift arrives.
Blue crabs shuffle
amid needle-width Saltgrass.
Ospreys, whistling like doormen for cabs,
dive for flounder.
Brackish pools stirred by egrets
that poke at three-spined-sticklebacks
underneath. So much we don't see.

Out of teeming mind of Creator
comes irrational exuberance of love,
procreative abandon.
Nature doubling & tripling itself.
Evil too, so sages say,
that wounds earth and people on it.

In distance, shovels grate stone as ditchers
drain mosquito breeding pools.
They needed jobs, the men,
but blue-wing teal ducks need larvae
to eat. At night, half-dazed ducks doze

on pond as though water mattress
and have necks snapped.
After, the men feast.

To get horse to walk on spongy

soil

wide wooden boards fit on hooves for
                              haying marsh grass.

The wind blows low, ruffling hay.
I smile, recall wife's husky voice at night.

I can't find sleep right now,
maybe later.
Maybe later as
Savannah Sparrows[9] fall silent.

9. A species of bird under threat by extinction.

Nexus

Simon avoided most cities. In them
he felt like hick, more, an alien.
Cities were centers for puppet masters.

Now two conscripts from Roman garrison
seized him as though public property.
He was to prop up stumbling prisoner.

At the place of the skull outside city
where the strong bury the weak with neither shovel
nor hand, but by power and precedent.

The two men lock eyes in shame for rebbe's rebuff
from crowd, its rejection of righteousness.
The men, adjoined by cross beam, a country
of two, an isthmus of joint self-giving.

POSTCHRI . . . .

Titanium tinsel
flutters at the future
over MoMA Bilbao.
Below,

Richard Serra's
earth-brown steel Walls
jail/warn/squeeze
you to life via panic attack.

the conversion of *Corpus Christi* church
into yet one more two-star restaurant

thus the cancelled christ
with el greco's resurrection
might as well be in
storage

Living with Grey's Anatomy

The Delta virus has infected my TV viewing.
I can't seem to sleep, if in episode, sex is withheld.
Will Karev play the hound or stay with Jo? Will Izzie cash
an 8.5 million check for falling for Denny D?
That's sex and money; what else is missing? Power . . . Yeah!
The series, more modern morality play than soap,
keeps me awake watching its whiplash-American plot.
The storyline has it all: genic terror and trauma;
        trailer trash who finally grab at the American Dream.
        The change to a post-racial, post-religious society
        explains how minorities own or run their hospitals,
        but why would one, as with-it, as nazi-chief, Miranda,
        suppose she had the need to pray before operating?
        I wonder if Preston Burke does *pro bono* work . . . yet?

Shabbat

dinner over.
keeping vigil for
candles' conclusion.
bay breeze alights,
then bounces.
smoke-crumble
spirals in orbit
beyond ceiling.

ancient sacrifice:
beeswax for light.
prophetic voice:
"He will not
quench
the sputtering
wick."

I vanishes
amid the
Presence.

A Monk's Aubade

He loved choir, the notion of a single note
from one worshipping brotherhood,
in monotone chants as from one throat.
He revered nave, and stalls, the graine'd wood.

> Before Prime he'd light each altar candle,
> walk down the hall to toll the call to prayer.
> We could hear the slapping of his sandal,
> followed by monks' procession down the stair.

Most of his long monastic life he farmed,
fathered rows of rutabagas and leeks,
shoveled rock and toppled trees to build the barn,
ran to Vespers on those summer weeks.

> I would often ask him for his counsel,
> (his humility was legendary
> at abbey) while praying in his bare cell,
> on the floor above the ossuary.

Fifty years a monk is but a half-life,
every breath attending a faithful God.
His was a habit of peace and non-strife,
Divine Office a daily fuel rod.

> His frame, bent and stretched over a lifetime,
> stooped by bows, the very vows he kept.
> He seemed more an antique bird roused at Prime,
> or a small sparrow fluttering on a step.

After Compline once he shuffled down the hall,
pulled by curve of spine and constancy.
In his cell, he'd dreamt he heard a call,
which filled his sleep somehow with ecstasy.

He'd loved the sun and morning Matins bell,
but couldn't wait for that day to break.
Something seemed to rise from him, he couldn't tell,
a lightness, unbound from life to wake.

Selfdonation

The hula of flame from son's birthday candle
spread around the table into every eye
looking at him get ready, lips puckered,
to send room into mock cosmic
darkness of 13 billion years ago.
Zuni myth[10] might tell of my child's descent
from dark pelvic cave into the blazing light.

Under penumbra of Great Salt Marsh,
nature's exhibition of lush fertility,
where shallow summer bays and estuaries
feed flounder and zooplankton
to nourish crabs, clams, electric eels,
even worms—which in turn feed duck and hawk
and Great Blue Heron—a Yahweh success story.

However, sullen shadows haunt the land.
Creator notices: wars of ambition;
Killing Fields; Hiroshima;
careless destruction of the earth;
the extinction of 93% of all species;
columns of 230,000
children heading to crematoria;
amid springtime beauty of verbena,

10. Anthropologists tell of a Zuni creation myth in which the people of the
Fourth World lived in eternal darkness until the Sun Father and his twin sons
took pity on them. They led those people out of their darkness towards intense
light which caused them to cry.

the viburnam shrub, the black oak,
the white blossomed yucca.

Our Father must have wondered
what had gone wrong after the serpent,
the apple, the Abel murder.
He'd devised a kind of water-meadow-
-kingdom of continual fulness.
Only later, developed personal paths from self-indulgence
to self-donation founded on Son's flogged flesh,
cauterized like God's branded lamb.
Either creation's design was flawed, he thought,
or man had bungled his Christian freedom.

The Shekinah midwifes the coming kingdom.
She is the perfecter, sanctifier, whisper
in prophets' ears. In Her freedom She nears
or disappears close to or far from holiness,
or its opposite.
Her thought is as agile as blue darter fish
in ponds. She binds, builds, births, bonds
our notions of righteousness, and laments
our selfish self-promotion.

The Creator sends Son into world
to open door for poor and ill.
The Father knew that love nullifies
hatred's darkness and chill.
First, Jesus builds a bonfire of pride,
washes feet, takes mockery in stride.
As Father recedes from Son's life,
Christ grieves His greatest loss.
Often, we make Him stand outside our door,
He who was once forced to wait upon a cross
burning for us, He a self-enkindled match,
waiting two thousand years or more.

Good-bye, Boomer

Went to computer shop last month.
The geek smiled at my blank boomer memory,
an infant's try, "goo . . . goo . . . google search."
The words jammed in my brain like bullets
in dirty chamber of a Glock.

Jesus predicted this—when you're old
someone will take you where you don't want to go.
Watching a former colleague in her nursing home,
I'm shocked how her Alzheimer's had raced ahead.
On waking she screams in fear all day,
as though she had been dumped in Kosovo.

Aging raises religious questions for me—
ontology, the nature of being.
Basic questions: Yahweh's "I AM WHO I AM."
Hamlet's "To be or not to be . . ."
which sounds more like, "Is a lie worth living with?"
Given that age subtracts life
decade by decade until
even I can't find the word
that I know I know.
Jesus offered his life to everyone
and his risen body to Christian supplicants—
"The bread I will give you for the life
of the world is my flesh,"
Spirit-haunted-breaded recurrence.
His life in exchange for Being,
that is the question.

Invitation List

The Sabbath feast will need chiefs of
neurology to help mystics waken
to Glory, chefs for the Banquet,
carvers of crutches and other
skilled craftsmen, assistants
who scurry about with pressed tux
under arm, junior and senior
partners under foot. However,
munition makers need not apply.
Food-shopping-carts for cardboard floor
with tarp, and more life-support stuff,
are no longer necessary.
See you on the other side and,
remember, bring invitation.